THE pencil book

loads of things
you can make or
do with a pencil

miri flower

photography by sara everett

Frances Lincoln Ltd
74–77 White Lion Street
London N1 9PF
www.franceslincoln.com

The Pencil Book
Copyright © Frances Lincoln 2014

First Frances Lincoln edition 2014

Produced for Frances Lincoln Ltd by editorsonline.org
and Tracy Killick Art Direction and Design

Miri Flower has asserted her right to be identified as the
author of this work in accordance with the Copyright,
Designs and Patents Act 1988 (UK).

A catalogue record for this book is available from the
British Library.

ISBN 978-0-7112-3584-7

Printed and bound in China

10 9 8 7 6 5 4 3 2 1

Please note that any reader or anyone in their charge
taking part in any of the activities described does so
at their own risk. Neither the author nor the publisher
can accept any legal responsibility for any harm,
injury, damage, loss or prosecution resulting from
the use or misuse of the activities, techniques, tools
or advice in the book.

contents

Discovering pencils 6

Inside and out 8
Make a viewfinder 10
Make a flower picture 11
Do some leaf rubbings 12
Make a mini windmill 14
Go on a nature walk 16
Make stone pictures 18
Make magical fairy folk 19
Make pencil boats 20
Capture some clouds 22

Pencil games 24
Play hangman 26
Play the doodle game 27
Play dots and boxes 28
Play quick-on-the-draw 29
Feed the birds 30
Play roll-a-colour 32
Make a fortune-teller 34
Play heads, bodies, feet 36
Play sprouts 38
Play pick-up sticks 39

Draw together 40
Take turns to draw 42
Make hidden pictures 44
Create crazy collages 45
Make plant-pot markers 46
Design a board game 48
Make promises 50
Hunt for treasure 51
Make a dot-to-dot puzzle 52
Make a menu 53
Make cookie-cutter cards 54
Make a friendship collage 56

Crafty pencils 58
Make pencil toppers 60
Make some valentines 62
Send a secret drawing 63
Make a pencil frame 64
Weave with pencils 65
Make a pencil pot 66
Make a spinning top 68
Build a pencil sculpture 69
Make a paper 'you' 70
Dress mini paper people 72
Make an arty hair clip 73
Make a travel holder 74
Cover your pencils 76
Make coins into pictures 77
Make a pencil mosaic 78

Doodles and drawings 80
Make a mini movie 82
Design a maze 84
Doodle forever 86
Make a mirror picture 87
Make your own map 88
Draw houses in blocks 90
Doodle in circles 91
Draw a portrait 92
Do a 3D drawing 94
Draw the other half 96
Draw your daydreams 98
Draw a few of your favourite things 99
Draw a mandala 100

Pencils plus 102
Stamp with your pencil! 104
Pencil-shaving craft 106
Make a chalky print 108
Make some scratch art 110
Create see-through art 112
Colour your family 113
Draw an optical illusion 114
Draw with erasers 116
Smudge it on purpose 117
Make a placemat 118
Spin some pencil art 120
Use dust for drawing 122

Pencil stuff 124
Index 126
Acknowledgments 128

discovering pencils

People have always loved to draw and leave their mark. From children drawing with sticks in the sand to artists drawing portraits, drawing is one of the oldest and most universal ways of creating a piece of art. However, sometimes it can be tricky to get started. This book is full of ideas and techniques for creating pictures, playing games and even making craft projects by recycling old pencils.

Use the ideas in this book as a starting point for your own artistic journey. I hope they will help you discover just how much you can do if you think creatively and take a chance. As you explore the ideas, remember that you don't need to end up with a perfect drawing or craft each time. It's all about experimenting. So don't get discouraged if things 'go wrong', because you will have simply created something else! Keep exploring the different ways in which you can make a picture, and, most importantly, have fun.

While many of the crafts in this book can be done with just pencils and paper alone, some need a few extra craft supplies. If you can, try to keep all your craft supplies in a special box or drawer, and always be on the look-out for things to add to your craft supply collection. You could ask your friends and family to help look out for things, too.

With all the projects in this book, follow the safety guidelines on page 124. Some activities are easy, while others are more challenging, and what is easy for one person may be tricky for another! The activity code (explained opposite) gives some guidance on levels of difficulty, but always take care when playing with pencils, as they are hard and sharp!

These may involve the use of tools (such as sharp scissors) or be fairly complicated, so are more suitable for older children.

These have some tricky sections which might require a little help from an adult.

These are easy things you can do on your own, and may be possible for very young children to do.

Glue sticks are easy to use even for little hands and are inexpensive.

Safety scissors are a useful thing to have in your collection of craft supplies. You never know when you might need to cut out a shape or snip a piece of wool.

Paper comes in a huge variety of colours and types, and you can really change the finished look of a project by using a different kind of paper. Look out for fairly traded or handmade paper, as this has a beautiful texture, but keep a supply of plain paper for doodles and sketches, too.

Notebooks can be useful for so many different things. Try carrying a small notebook and pencil with you always, to capture your ideas.

Natural materials such as dried leaves, sticks, clean feathers, seashells and pebbles are a wonderful addition to many crafts, and will help connect you to the world around you.

Recycled materials like bottle tops, cereal boxes or old buttons often come in handy. In our home we have a big basket full of these fun craft things, because you never know when you might need to add something special to a project.

Crafty bits like googly eyes, bits of foam and pipe-cleaners are great to use for final touches. Try to keep a few things like this in your craft box.

1

inside and out

01 make a viewfinder

Sometimes it's hard to choose what to draw from all the things around you, especially outside. A viewfinder will help you see what will look good in a frame.

- Find a piece of sturdy card, such as the side of a cereal box.

- Cut out a square, roughly 10 x 10 cm (4 x 4 inches).

- Fold the square card in half and then cut out a small square (with rounded edges, if you like) from the folded edge, so that when you unfold your card there is a hole in the centre.

- Hold up your viewfinder about 30 cm (12 inches) from your face and use it to look around you. When you're ready to draw, close one eye, look through the hole and draw what you see!

make a flower picture

Flower petals make a really pretty addition to a drawing. In summer, it's easy to use pressed flower petals, but if you want to do this in winter, you could use leaves or thin fabric petals in pretty colours.

● Collect some flower petals. Dry and flatten them by putting them between two sheets of paper and then placing the paper under a heavy book for a few hours.

● When they are ready, use a glue stick to carefully glue the petals to a sheet of paper.

● Make them into pictures by using colouring pencils to add details around them. For instance, you could add long trails to make them into balloons, or draw a person around them, so the petals become a beautiful dress.

do some leaf rubbings

Leaf rubbings are fun to do and if you combine them with bark rubbings, even young children can create a picture of a tree. You will need some dry leaves, a piece of bark, some paper and some soft colouring pencils.

● Place your bark on a firm surface and cover it with a piece of paper. Gently rub a brown pencil across the surface of the paper where the bark is to create the trunk of your finished tree.

● Arrange some leaves underneath the paper and rub green, red or orange pencils gently over the paper where they are.

Place your bark in a warm laundry area for a couple of days or even bake it in an oven to make sure it is completely dry.

04

make a mini windmill

Pencil windmills are fun on a windy day and look great as decorations on flowerpots. All you need is some thin card (or sturdy paper), a pencil, scissors and a push-pin.

● Cut your card into a square. Fold the square diagonally, first one way, then the other. Open up the card and cut halfway along the fold lines, from the outside corner towards the centre.

● Turn down every other corner, pointing each one towards the middle of your square, to create the blades of your windmill.

● Fix the paper blades to your pencil with the push-pin. You might like to ask an adult to help with this.

You can use colourful card or draw your own design onto the card. If you want to use your windmill as a bird scarer in a vegetable plot, choose bright, scary colours!

go on a nature walk

Sometimes it's fun to go for a walk armed with your pencil and a notebook – all the great explorers did this. If you do this regularly, you'll really notice the seasonal changes.

Find a quiet spot in a garden or park and observe the things around you. You might see a bird or an old tree stump, or even some beetles or a snail.

Draw what you can see. Don't worry about being able to create a perfect likeness, because these drawings are just for you. You can draw your whole view or just focus on one thing, such as a gnarly piece of bark or an oddly shaped rock.

Look for interesting details, like the spidery veins on a leaf or odd markings on stones.

06 make stone pictures

Stones can provide a great surface for your drawings. There are lots to choose from and they are free. Next time you visit a park or pebbly beach, collect some smooth, pale stones or pebbles. Make sure that you are allowed to take them home with you, because some areas are protected or belong to somebody.

Use bright pencils to draw pictures onto the stones. You can keep all your stones in a little pouch and turn them into story stones, too! Just close your eyes, pick a few stones and then make up a story that includes all of the items on the stones.

make magical fairy folk

Use your imagination to create your very own flower fairy or elf. All you will need are some pressed flower petals, some thin card and some colouring pencils.

● Collect flower petals and flatten them between two sheets of paper under a heavy book for a few hours. You can also use fabric flower petals for this project.

● Draw a tiny person onto your card. Give him or her some hair, a face, and some clothes.

● Cut out your person, then attach a flower petal as a dress, skirt, cape or even a hat! If you want to make your people into puppets, simply glue each one onto the top of a pencil.

In the winter, you can use fabric petals instead of real, pressed ones. Experiment with evergreen leaves too.

08

make pencil boats

Boats are really fun to play with, and these pencil boats are perfect for racing on puddles or streams. All you need is some card, glue, scissors and a pencil.

- Fold your card in half, then draw the outline of a boat onto the paper so that the bottom of the boat lies along the fold. This will ensure that no water will get into your boat. The boat shape can be as simple as a crescent shape.

- Cut out your shape and glue or tape the sides together to make a boat.

- Use a generous amount of glue to secure your pencil to the inside of the boat, to create a mast. If you like, you can also add a flag to the mast.

Try making several boats from different materials and see which one can sail for longest without sinking, or have a race with your friends!

09

capture some clouds

Clouds are amazing – they often look like strange animals or objects, and no two ever look alike. Try drawing a few special clouds to remember them.

- Find a blank notebook and some colouring pencils.

- On a day when you can see clouds, go outside and look up into the sky. If you spot a cloud that looks like something interesting, draw it in your notebook.

- Use your pencils to add fun details, such as a ball of wool for a cat-shaped cloud, or a handle for a dark, umbrella-shaped cloud. If you like, you can also add the date and the name of the place you were standing when you spotted the cloud.

Make a simple notebook by folding some sheets of paper within a slightly larger sheet, making two holes and tying it all together with a ribbon.

2

pencil games

10 play hangman

Hangman is a word game for as many players as you like. It is easy to learn, quick to play, and great when you're travelling. All you need is some paper and a pencil.

● Think of a secret word and draw a dash for each letter of the word onto the piece of paper (so you would draw _ _ _ _ if your secret word is four letters long).

● Ask the other players to take turns to guess what letters are in the word. If a player guesses a letter correctly, write it onto the dashed line where it belongs. If a player suggests a letter that is not in your word, draw one section of the hangman (like the one shown above).

● Players can keep guessing until the word is complete or the hangman is fully drawn. If the other players guess the word before you have drawn the whole hangman, they win. If you complete the hangman before the word is guessed, you win!.

play the doodle game

The doodle game is fun to play alone or with friends. All you need is some paper and pencils. Start with each player drawing a few funny shapes onto a piece of paper. Then swap the pieces of paper and look at the shapes. What can you add to turn these doodles into drawings? Could that doodle be an enormous tree, or a wizard's house?

After you have turned all the doodles into drawings, show them to each other and compare. It's fascinating to see what the other player made from your doodle.

For best results, give yourself a few minutes to look at the doodle before turning it into a drawing.

12

play dots and boxes

This game is a favourite for lots of children, all around the world. It is played on a square grid, which you can draw up if you don't have any grid-type notepaper. You will also need two colouring pencils.

● Create a play area on your paper by drawing several rows of evenly spaced dots.

● Take turns in drawing a line to connect two dots. Make sure each player uses a different colour pencil. When a player 'closes' a square, colour it in using that player's colour, and let that player draw another line. When the whole play area has been coloured in, the player with the most squares wins.

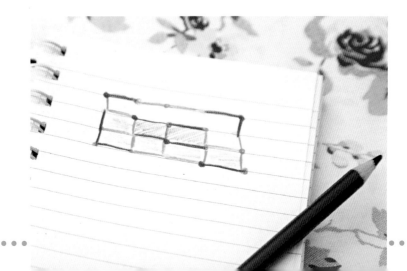

Another way to play is to write one word on lots of cards, then take turns to pull a card and draw the word written on it.

play quick-on-the-draw

This game will test your ability to draw under pressure. You can play with as many people as you like and all you need is a pencil and two pieces of paper.

● Sit next to a friend and think of a word that will be easy to draw. Start to draw the word.

● Your friend has to guess what it is you are drawing. If they can guess it before you finish the drawing, they get a point.

● Now it's your friend's turn to draw and your turn to guess.

● When you have finished playing the game, colour in your drawings together.

14 feed the birds

In this game for two players, you must guess where your friend has hidden his birds and throw fish at them to feed them. You will need paper and colouring pencils.

● Start by creating your 'ponds'. Do this by drawing up a large grid of squares, making sure that you both draw the same number of squares (perhaps six across and six down).

● Decide how many birds to have on the grid and what sizes

they are. For instance, on a grid of 36 squares, you could hide seven different sized birds and still leave plenty of blanks, by using: four small birds that take up one square, two that take up two squares, and one huge bird that takes up three or four squares. Draw your agreed choice of birds onto your grids.

● Now take turns to guess where the other player's birds are hidden. For example, you could say "I throw a fish at the first square in the second row!" Your friend will then draw a fish into that space on his pond. If you hit or 'feed' a bird, you get another go; if you miss, it is your friend's turn. The winner is whoever feeds all the birds on the other person's paper.

15

play roll-a-colour

There is no limit to the number of players for this competitive game, so it's great for birthday parties or family game nights. You will need paper, colouring pencils and a dice with different coloured sides or dots.

● Start by drawing the outline of a simple picture that can be coloured in using only the six colours on the dice. It might be a house with a path lined by trees, with a glowing sun overhead. Each player can now copy this drawing onto their paper or you can photocopy the drawing for each player.

● Players take it in turns to roll the dice, beginning with the youngest player. The colour rolled on the dice is the colour you fill in on your drawing – so if you roll and red is uppermost on the dice, colour in the part of your drawing that you think would normally be red (perhaps red roof tiles?).

● If you forget to colour a part of your picture, you will need to wait until you roll that colour again. The first person to colour in their whole picture is the winner.

16

make a fortune-teller

This little piece of paper might not really be able to tell you the future, but it is really fun to play with. You will need a square piece of paper and some pencils.

● Start by folding your paper in half. Push down on the folded edge to crease the paper. Then fold it in half again.

● Now unfold the paper and fold it diagonally each way to create more creases. When you unfold your paper, the creases should now make a star shape.

● Starting with the paper flat, fold each corner towards the centre of the paper, (the centre of all your creases) then flip over your paper without unfolding it.

● Now fold each corner of your already-folded paper towards the centre. You now have four flaps, divided into a total of eight sections.

● Lift up each flap, and draw a 'fortune' (such as a sports trophy or a microphone for a pop star) onto each section.

● When you have finished drawing, fold over the flaps again and mark each of the eight sections now showing with different colours. You can scribble, stamp or mark with colour in any way you like – the colours just need to be visible.

● Bring the corners of your fortune-teller up together so that it becomes a 3D shape. Gently open up the outer sections to create room for your fingers, and put your thumb and first finger from each hand into the four flaps.

● Ask a friend to choose a number between one and ten. Now open and close your fortune-teller that many times, by pulling it open forwards then sideways, back and forth, like a bird's beak that opens both ways. After the right number of times, ask your friend to pick one of the colours now showing. Open and close the fortune-teller again, spelling out the letters of the colour – e.g. R–E–D. Then ask your friend to pick a colour again. Take out your fingers, lift the flap, and you'll see their fortune!

17

play heads, bodies, feet

Fold-over drawings often end up being really silly pictures that will make you and your friends laugh. All you need for this game is some paper and pencils.

● Each player starts by drawing a head at the top of their paper. This can be the head of anything – a person, an animal, or even a monster. Add two lines beneath it for a neck, then fold the paper backwards until only the neck lines are visible.

● Pass the paper on to the next player, who then draws the upper body onto the neck without peeking at the head, and leaves some lines 'poking out' to show where to start the lower body. Keep passing on the drawings until they are finished.

play sprouts

This popular strategy game starts with just a few dots, but it quickly grows into a brilliant game.

● Start by drawing a few dots onto a piece of paper. The more dots you draw, the longer and trickier the game will be. Four dots is a good number to start with.

● The first player now connects any two dots, using either a curved or straight line. He or she then adds a new dot somewhere on the line just drawn. The next player does the same, and so on. No one's line can cross any other line, and no dot can have more than three lines running into or away from it. The player who runs out of lines to draw loses the game.

Although sprouts was invented by two mathematicians – John Conway and Michael Paterson – it is quick and easy to learn.

play pick-up sticks

Everyone loves to play pick-up sticks, and if you and your friends have lots of pencils, you already have everything you need for a game at any time!

Decide on a few different colours of pencils to use and assign each colour a different value. For instance, an orange pencil might be worth five points, a blue one only two.

Hold all your pencils together in one hand and then open your hand to let the pencils fall. Take turns trying to pick up a pencil without moving any of the other pencils. If another pencil moves, it is the next player's go. When all the pencils have been picked up, add up your points. The player with the most points wins.

3

draw together

20

take turns to draw

While it is fun to draw pictures by yourself, it is even more fun to draw together. To do this, all you need is some paper, colouring pencils and another person!

● Start by deciding on a theme for your drawing. Will it be serious or funny? Realistic or a fantasy world?

● The first person draws one part of the picture, such as a tree.

● The other person adds to the picture – perhaps adding a bird to the tree, for example.

● Keep taking turns to add things or just start drawing together until you both feel that the drawing is finished.

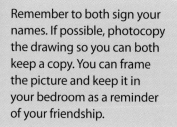

Remember to both sign your names. If possible, photocopy the drawing so you can both keep a copy. You can frame the picture and keep it in your bedroom as a reminder of your friendship.

make hidden pictures

These folding pictures are a great way to surprise your friends, because one picture turns into another. All you need is some paper and colouring pencils.

● Fold your paper into thirds, crease it and unfold it again. You now have two side sections and one centre section. Lift up one of the side sections and fold it back on itself. Then do the same to the other side section. Your paper should now look a bit like a cupboard with closed doors.

● Draw a simple picture onto the front of your drawing, across the two doors. Then unfold the paper completely and find a way to turn the two halves of your drawing into the outer edges of one large drawing. Close the doors again to hide the big picture.

create crazy collages

This is a game for players of all ages and for as many players as you like. All you need are one or two pieces of paper for each player and some colouring pencils.

● The first player thinks of a word and says it out loud for everyone to hear, such as 'castle'. Everyone draws the word.

● The next player thinks of another word, such as 'goldfish'. Now all the players have to include that item in their drawing. One person might draw a goldfish in a pond, another might draw a goldfish-shaped balloon floating in the sky. Keep taking turns, naming and adding items to your pictures. Everyone will end up with a very different picture that tells a unique story.

make plant-pot markers

Plant-pot markers make a lovely present for anyone who likes to grow flowers, herbs or vegetables. They are easy to make but look great, and all you need is some paper, pencils and a glue stick. Unless you want to give them a flower too, of course!

● Fold a piece of paper in half, and draw a very long rectangle (about 2.5 x 6 cm or 1 x 2½ inches) with a 'blob' at one end, so the whole thing looks like a very long toe.

● Draw a colourful picture of a flower or plant on the blob.

● Now cut out the whole shape. As you're using folded paper, you will have two identical shapes. Run a glue stick up the edges of the long shape and all over the blob, then stick the two pieces together. You should still have a pocket for inserting a pencil. Put the pencil inside and plant it in a pot!

24

design a board game

Board games are lots of fun, but wouldn't it be even more fun if you were in charge of making the rules? All you need is some paper, sturdy card and some pencils.

Start by drawing a starting point and a finishing point onto your card. Then connect those two places by drawing a wiggly path made of stepping stones. Now you can add extra things to some of the little steps along the way – like a puddle that makes you lose a turn, or a pond that requires you to roll a certain number to cross. Decorate your game board however you like, adding details like trees or animals. Glue your paper onto the sturdy card. If you like, put a larger piece of card underneath your game and bend it up around the edges to stop the dice rolling away.

25 make promises

If you are looking for a great homemade present for friends or family, you could surprise them with a whole stack of 'promises' on homemade coupons. These work best on special types of paper such as handmade or highly textured paper.

- Use scissors to cut your paper into rectangles, or tear the edges carefully to make the coupons look even more special.

- Draw pictures of the things you want to give to people onto the rectangles. These could be treats (like ice cream) or events (like a trip to the park) or promises of things you'll do (like tidy your room or give that person a hug).

hunt for treasure

It's fun to hide little presents or items for your friends then give them a map so they can find what you have hidden. You can use off-white paper to make your map feel like a real, old treasure map, if you like.

● Decide whether to hide the treasure inside or outside. Then draw the starting point (such as the kitchen table) and the treasure hiding place ('X') onto your piece of paper.

● Connect the two places by drawing different spots along the way to guide the treasure seekers – such as a gate (outside), or mum's computer (inside). If you want, you can scrunch up your paper and unfold it again to make your map seem older.

Remember to ask permission before hiding anything or going outside.

27

make a dot-to-dot puzzle

Dot-to-dot pictures are fun to solve and really easy to make. You can create your own with just a few pencils, some sturdy card and some paper.

Start by drawing and cutting out a shape – such as a giraffe – from your piece of card. Put the card on top of a piece of paper. Go around the card, making dots all around the shape on the paper. These will be the dots to connect, so make them closer for young children and further apart for older children and adults.

Remove your card from the paper and add some details to the picture, such as trees or other animals.

Make sure it is possible to connect all the dots with one line before giving your dot-to-dot puzzle to a friend to complete.

make a menu

Have you always wanted to own a restaurant or be a chef? Draw a pretend restaurant menu and invite your friends or family over for a pretend meal. All you need is several pieces of paper or card and some pencils.

● Fold each of your paper pieces (or card) in half, to create folding menus.

● Think of some delicious meals, snacks and drinks. If this is a pretend meal, be adventurous! You might want to include some new, funny food creations like gummy-bear soup or chocolate spaghetti. Draw pictures of the food items onto the menus.

● Invite your friends or family to your pretend restaurant. You can set the table and practise your waiting skills while they choose what to order from your handmade menus.

29

make cookie-cutter cards

This is a great way to use up scraps of scribbled paper from projects that didn't turn out quite right. If you have some cookie cutters, thick paper, glue, scissors and pencils, you can make beautiful greetings cards using those valuable scraps of scribbled paper.

- Start by putting the cookie cutters onto the scribbled paper, then draw around them. If you don't have any scrap paper, you could doodle on a new piece of paper or card and then draw around cookie cutters on that.

- Cut out the shapes using your scissors.

- Fold another piece of thick paper or card in half to create a greetings card. You might want to play around with your shapes on the front of the card for a while, to decide where each one looks best. When you're happy with the design, use a glue stick to attach your shapes onto the front of the card.

- Add any decorations that you like. Glitter is always good on a Christmas card!

30

make a friendship collage

Celebrate your friendship and all the things that make your friends unique by creating a paper friendship collage together. You will need one really large piece of paper (such as easel paper or wallpaper lining), some pieces of card, paints and a paintbrush, colouring pencils and glue.

● Cut the card into small, square pieces and give one to each of your friends. Ask them to draw something they love or something that is special about them onto their square. Ask them to write their name and age onto the back of the card too.

● Use paint and a paintbrush to paint the large sheet of paper in a bright colour and let it dry completely.

● Use a glue stick to glue your friends' pictures onto the large piece of paper. You might want to put their name and age next to the cards so you can see who drew what. Don't forget to design a square for yourself, too!

● Display the collage in your room.

4

crafty pencils

31

make pencil toppers

Pencil toppers are an easy way to make boring-looking pencils look more interesting and to personalise them. To make your own pencil toppers, you will need some craft foam, pencils, glue, scissors and googly eyes.

- Start by drawing your design onto the craft foam. Flowers and animals are easy to draw, so they are often a good start.

- Cut out your design with scissors.

- Place the design on top of some more craft foam and draw round it. Then cut out the second shape. The two shapes should be identical.

- Now stick the two shapes together with the top of a pencil between them. When the glue is dry, you can decorate your pencil toppers with stickers, googly eyes or glitter glue!

If you want to, you could use the pencil toppers as puppets and then put on a show for your friends and family.

32 make some valentines

These pencil valentines are so quick and easy that you can make lots of them. That way no one feels left out! You will need a pencil and some card, feathers and glue.

- Cut a heart shape from your card, to any size you like.

- Cut two slits into the paper for your pencil. You might need some help with this part.

- Slide the pencil through the slits in the heart.

- Now decorate the pencil to look like an arrow. You can add an arrow tip by glueing a paper triangle to the tip, or you could glue feathers to the other end. Then decide whether to sign the card or not. Do you want your identity to remain a secret?

send a secret drawing

This is a brilliant way to surprise someone – especially if they like solving codes and puzzles. All you will need is some paper, pencils and lemon juice.

● Pour some lemon juice into a shallow dish. Dip the top end of your pencil into the lemon juice and start drawing your picture using just the lemon juice, as if it were ink.

● While the juice is still wet and you can see it, add some details with the 'normal' end of your pencils to provide clues about the finished picture (like the apples on a tree).

● To reveal the hidden drawing, your friend will need to bake the paper in an oven until the lemon juice turns brown. Then he or she can colour in the whole picture and give it back to you!

34

make a pencil frame

Why not make a pencil picture frame to let everyone know how creative you are? You will need pencils, glue and an old picture frame.

- Arrange pencils on two opposite sides of the frame. Then lay pencils on the other two sides, overlapping at the corners. It is easiest if all your pencils are the same length, but if they are not you can just move things around a little bit to make them fit.

- Remove all the pencils from the frame, but remember where they belong. You could arrange them on a piece of paper alongside your frame to help you remember.

- Now cover your frame with glue and stick your pencils into place, using those for the bottom layer first. Press down onto the pencils to make sure they stick firmly to the frame.

weave with pencils

This beautiful object is inspired by the traditional weavings of the Huichol people of Mexico. You will need two pencils and some string or colourful wool.

● Hold your pencils together in a cross shape and tie them together with one end of your string or wool. It might be easier to ask someone for help with this part, as it can be quite tricky.

● Now start to weave, looping over and under the arms of the cross, one by one, in a clockwise direction. Keep going until your design reaches the size you want.

● If you want a brightly coloured weaving, you can use rainbow coloured wool or lots of pieces of different coloured wool tied together to wrap your pencils. When it's finished, you can display your weaving on a wall or hang it in a window.

36

make a pencil pot

This fun little pot is a great place to store your favourite pencils and it is like a magic trick – it looks as though all your pencils have found a way to stand up on their own! You will need a tubular cardboard box (like the ones used for biscuits or crisps), a glue stick and lots of colourful pencils.

● Completely cover the outside of the tube with glue.

● Stand it on a firm surface, like a table or chopping board, and start attaching your pencils to the tube, one by one. Don't leave any gaps as you work your way around the tube.

● Let your pot dry and then fill it with your favourite pens and pencils. Or give it to a friend to brighten up their desk.

By using different containers and different heights of pencils you can make pots of differing sizes. Try making one-colour pots too!

37 make a spinning top

It's easy to make pencils into little 'spinning people' by decorating them with things from your craft box. You will need a pencil, some tissue paper, wool, pipe-cleaners and a glue stick.

● Cut out a strip of tissue paper and attach it to the lower half of your pencil with glue, allowing it to stick out like a ballerina's tutu. If you want to make a spinning man, cut out a pair of trousers with legs apart, as though your man is star-jumping.

● Pull apart some wool and stick it to the pencil as hair. Then stick a round paper 'face' on top, and draw in eyes and a mouth.

● Wrap a pipe-cleaner around the pencil to give your person arms and a body. Then stand your pencil onto a piece of paper and spin it like a spinning top. This makes a great gift, too.

build a pencil sculpture

You can build interesting structures and sculptures using nothing but pencils and modelling clay. The more pencils and clay you have, the bigger your final sculpture can be.

- Roll a small piece of modelling clay into a ball.

- Stick a pencil into the clay and put another small ball of clay onto the other end.

- Use more clay balls to connect lots of pencils to each other.

- You can build houses, abstract shapes or even people. If you use air-drying clay, you can make structures that last forever.

make a paper 'you'

Have you ever wanted to visit friends or relatives who live too far away to visit? Why not make a paper version of yourself so you can send your paper 'you' on exciting adventures? You will need a piece of paper big enough to draw a large picture of yourself, some pencils and scissors.

● If you want to make a life-size version of yourself, ask a friend to draw around your body while you are lying on the piece of paper. If you are making the paper 'you' yourself, draw your body onto a piece of paper at any size that you like.

● Decorate your shape by adding hair, colourful clothes, a face and any other details that will help other people to recognise that the paper person is a 2D copy of you!

● Now you need to cut out the body shape. Remember to be especially careful when cutting out your fingers, as they can be quite fiddly.

● Choose who to send it to. Your grandparents would love receiving a paper version of their grandchild in the post, so they might be your first choice. Or give it to your parents, and make a paper 'you' once a year to show how much you have grown.

40

dress mini paper people

Paper people are fun toys and you can make them look however you like. You will need paper, pencils and scissors.

● Draw a 'person' shape onto a piece of paper, then carefully cut it out. Draw a face and some underwear onto the paper person.

● Put the shape onto a new piece of paper, and trace around the body to create an outline for clothes. Draw a few small tabs onto the clothes – these will stick out when you cut out the clothes, and you can then fold them onto your paper person.

● Colour the clothes then cut them out, keeping the tabs.

● Use the little tabs to attach the clothes to your mini people. Add some finishing touches using wool, fabric or buttons.

You can also decorate the pencil with glitter or use more than one pencil.

make an arty hair clip

This pencil hair clip makes a great gift, especially for teachers, who always want to have a pencil handy! You will need an old hair clip, a tiny, used pencil, and PVA glue.

● Wipe your pencil and hair clip with a cloth to remove any dirt or dust. This will help them to stick to each other.

● Apply a small blob of PVA glue to the end of your hair clip.

● Carefully place your little pencil in the glue. Wait until the glue is dry before testing out the clip on your own hair!

42

make a travel holder

This easy-to-make pencil holder is a great way to take your pencils with you wherever you go. You will need an A4 sheet of felt, some string and scissors.

● Use scissors to cut two small slits, one above the other, into the piece of felt, about halfway down from the top. (You might want to ask an adult to help you with this step.) It is easiest to cut the felt if you fold it in half and then cut small slits on the fold. Practise on some paper first if you feel unsure about where to make the cuts.

● Make a series of these cuts all along the felt, about 2 cm (½ inch) apart. Then slide the pencils into the holes. Add some string, or a ribbon or even some plaited wool to wrap around your pencil holder and keep it closed.

43 cover your pencils

This is an easy way to turn boring-looking pencils into interesting ones. All you need is some colourful paper, a rubber band, scissors, a glue stick and some old pencils.

- Pick up the colourful paper and cut out a rectangle that is as tall as your pencil.

- Cover the back of the paper with glue. Wrap the paper around the pencil and secure it with a rubber band. When the glue is dry, remove the rubber band and cut away any excess paper.

- If you want to give someone a secret message, write it on the back of some colourful paper then wrap the paper tightly around the pencil, using only a little blob of glue at the end. Use the rubber band to hold it in place while the glue dries.

76

make coins into pictures

Do you have a collection of coins from your holidays? You can turn them into a wonderful holiday keepsake with just some paper and pencils.

● Put the coins onto a firm surface, arranging them in a way that would look good on a picture. You might want to put coins from the same country together. Then cover the coins with a sheet of paper.

● Gently rub your pencil over the paper where the coins are. Use different coloured pencils for different coins, if you want to. The outlines and pictures on the coins will start to appear on the paper as if by magic!

You could also cut out the paper coins to use as pretend money in some of your games.

45

make a pencil mosaic

Drawing is not the only way to make a picture with pencils – you can use the pencils themselves in a mosaic. You will need some pencils, a pencil sharpener, a canvas or piece of card, and a glue stick.

● Think of a design for your pencils, such as a heart shape. Square things like houses or spiky things like palm trees are the easiest to make. Test out your design by arranging pencils of different lengths into the shape you want, using a sharpener to change the lengths or sharpen both ends, if you need to.

● When you have arranged the pencils as you want them, cover one side of each pencil with glue and stick it into place. Press down gently onto the finished design.

5 doodles

and drawings

46

make a mini movie

It is fun to watch movies at the cinema, but it is even more fun to make a movie yourself. This project uses drawings to trick your brain into thinking that the picture is actually moving. You will need some paper and pencils, scissors, a hole-punch and some string.

● Start by using scissors to cut a piece of paper into little pages for your book. You might want anything from 10 to 25 pages.

● Stack all the pieces of paper on top of each other and make sure they are all the same size.

● Now begin drawing your movie. Simply draw a picture into the bottom right-hand corner of each page, making sure each picture is only a little bit different from the previous one. If you have drawn a man walking, alternate the leg that is sticking out in front – left on the first page, right on the second, left on the third, and so on. If you are drawing a seed growing into a flower, draw it emerging slightly more on each page.

● When you have finished drawing, use the hole-punch to create two holes in the left-hand side of the stack and then tie some string through the holes to make a little book. If the book has only a few pages, you could staple it together instead.

● Flick through the book pages with your thumb as quickly as possible. It will look as though you are watching a little movie of ever-changing pictures.

design a maze

When you design your own maze you can make it as tricky or easy as you like, and decorate it to be in your favourite colours or themes. Why not make a football maze? All you need is some paper, an eraser and a pencil.

● Mark the starting point and the finishing point for the maze onto your piece of paper.

● Connect the two spots by drawing a 'tube' that curves and wiggles all around your paper.

● Now you need to add some 'wrong ways' off the tube to confuse players. Use your eraser to rub out some gaps at certain places on the tube, and draw new tubes leading away from the main one, curling around the paper and eventually running off the edge.

● Test your maze to make sure that there is only one way from the start to the finish. Colour in your tubes to make your maze more colourful and then try it out on your friends.

48

doodle forever

This is a great way to fill some time if you are feeling bored. It's an experiment with patterns, and you can draw it as small or as large as you want to. You'll need some coloured pencils and some paper.

Use a dark pencil to draw a line onto a piece of paper. Let the line swirl around the paper and cross over itself at many points before drawing it back to where it started. The larger you make the overall pattern and the more times you make the line cross itself, the longer your pattern will take to fill. Now colour in each segment with a different colour or pattern.

If you finish drawing but have more time to spare, add to the pattern by picking a starting point and swirling the line outside your original pattern.

make a mirror picture

You don't need a copying machine to create copies of your pictures – all you need is some paper, a pencil and a small hand mirror. This is a great way to copy even complicated drawings, but start with an easy one to learn the technique.

- Draw a simple picture onto the left-hand side of a piece of paper, such as a car. If you are left-handed, draw on the right.

- Put a hand mirror onto the paper, next to the picture. Slant the top of the mirror slightly away from the picture, and look directly down onto the mirror. Let your eyes glaze slightly, and you will suddenly see your picture on the clean side of the paper.

- Use a pencil to trace over the lines you can see. Notice that if you shut one eye, the image disappears!

make your own map

Maps are ways of discovering new places, which may be real or fantasy. Why not try drawing your own map, of your neighbourhood or school, or somewhere more fantastic, like a prehistoric dinosaur world or a fairytale land? All you need is some paper and colouring pencils.

- Start by drawing the most important places onto your map (which might be your home, the dinosaur's cave or a gingerbread house!).

- Now add interesting landmarks around this world, such as roads, streams, parks, mountains, forests, cliffs and oceans.

- Finally, add details such as people, animals, trees and plants to your map.

- If you like, you can scrunch up your paper gently then unfold it again. This will add creases to your map and make it look old and used.

51

draw houses in blocks

Next time you go for a walk, look at all the different shapes that are used in building houses. You will find circles, cubes, squares, triangles, pyramids and more. Why not try designing your own house from just a few basic shapes? You just need some paper and pencils.

Start by thinking of a design for your house. Draw the basic structure of the house using shapes like big squares or rectangles. Add a triangle as the roof. When you have finished drawing the outline of the house, decorate it with unusual features, such as circle-shaped windows or star-shaped doors.

doodle in circles

This drawing technique is an easy doodle that creates amazing pictures. Mathematicians call them 'Apollonian gaskets' and they are made from groups of circles.

● Start by drawing a shape onto a piece of paper. Triangles are easy, so a large triangle is a good way to start.

● Now draw the biggest circle you can possibly fit into the triangle. Drawing the circle will create more areas outside it, where you can draw more circles.

● Keep drawing the biggest circle you can into the spaces you create. Colour them in with bright colours. Then try out different shapes and see what they look like filled with circles.

53

draw a portrait

This project shows you how to surprise someone with a hand-drawn portrait that they will want to keep forever, because you drew it! All you need is a printed photo of the person you want to draw, some lightweight paper and some colouring pencils.

- Place your piece of paper on top of the photograph.

- Start by tracing the outline of the person's head shape, then trace their eyes, eyebrows, hairline, mouth, nose and neck onto your picture.

- Now add details to the face, such as eyelashes, freckles and so on.

- When you have finished adding the details, start colouring in the person.

- Now add a background to the portrait. Choose a colour they like or something that reflects them and their tastes. If your dad loves music, for instance, you could draw him on stage!

do a 3D drawing

People will be amazed by this 3D illusion, which you can create in just a few simple steps. You will need a piece of paper, a ruler and some pencils in different colours.

● Start by gently tracing around any object you want to use. (Your foot is a great place to start.) As you draw around it, press the pencil very lightly – you do not want this line to be visible in the finished picture.

● Now use different-coloured pencils to draw straight lines that run from the edges of the paper (left and right) to where your foot outline begins. Do not draw inside the foot shape. Leave a small space between the lines as you draw.

● Now connect the lines on either side of your foot, by drawing a slightly arched line each time, as shown (left).

● Once you have finished drawing the lines, colour in the space between the lines with bright colours, colouring from one side of the paper right over to the other side, including the foot.

● It will look as though your foot is raised on the paper!

draw the other half

Most days we receive some sort of catalogue or brochure in the post. It is such a shame to simply recycle these things, so here is a fun use for all those colourful pictures. All you need is a printed picture, some paper and some colouring pencils.

Pick an image from the brochure or catalogue that you like and cut it out. (Remember always to ask permission before you cut out anything.)

Cut the image in half or pick a particularly interesting section of the image. Glue that part onto a piece of paper. Use your imagination to finish the picture with a pencil drawing.

56

draw your daydreams

We all like daydreaming, even if it's just imagining being on a warm beach when the weather outside is cold and wet. Why not make pictures of your daydreams, so you can go there in an instant?

● Ask an adult to print out one of your holiday pictures onto drawing paper, or choose a picture in a catalogue or magazine.

● Add fun details to the picture using your coloured pencils. Draw balloons or kites in the sky, for instance, or add a big ship or sea monster to the water.

● You can print and draw lots of different pictures and keep them in a special album or art journal.

draw a few of your favourite things

We all feel sad sometimes, and at those times it's great to have something that instantly makes you feel better. A happiness journal is a collection of things that make you feel happy. All you need is a notebook and some pencils.

Every time something makes you smile, draw a picture of it in your happiness journal. You could get into the habit of drawing in here daily, sketching all the good things that happened to you during the day. But use your imagination too – if it makes you smile, draw it.

58

draw a mandala

Mandalas are circular drawings that start in the middle and spread outwards. They are easy to design and all you need is some paper and colouring pencils.

- Think of a theme for your mandala. You can draw animals, fruit or just simple shapes and swirls.

- First, draw a small picture – such as a tomato – in the middle of your paper.

- Now draw a circle of things (such as bananas) around it.

- Keep letting your drawing grow outwards by adding more and more circles of little pictures, all relating to the same theme.

- Your mandala is finished whenever you feel it is complete.

6

pencils plus

59

stamp with your pencil!

Lots of pencils have round erasers on one end, and these little circles make perfect paint stamps. All you need is a pencil with an eraser, some paper and watercolour paints.

- Start by wetting the eraser of your pencil in a small cup of water. Then rub it gently over the watercolour paint.

- Now use the eraser of your pencil as a stamp. You can pre-draw designs and follow the outline with your stamping pencil, or you can simply use the little dots you produce as a way of creating pictures from scratch.

- Use lots of different colours. You can make any picture or shape you want. This technique is a great way to make invitations or design your own stationery.

- Try out a variety of colour combinations and don't be afraid to think big. You can't go wrong when you are being creative!

pencil-shaving craft

The curly pencil shavings that fall from your pencil when you sharpen it can be used to make really unusual pictures with lots of texture. All you need are some pencils, paper, a pencil sharpener and a glue stick.

● Start by picking a few pencils that have interesting patterns or vivid colours on the outside – up the length of the pencil – because these are the colours that will edge each of your pencil shavings. You might like to experiment with different sharpeners too, because the shavings will differ in size and thickness.

Pencil shavings are great for giving a drawing of a bald man some funny hair, or a sheep lots of wool, or for designing a ball gown with layers and layers of frilly shavings.

● Sharpen your pencils and carefully collect the shavings – they are quite fragile!

● Draw a picture that might be fun to decorate with pencil shavings. You could use a single piece for the tutu of a ballerina, or lots of pencil shavings for the scales of a fantastic fish!

make a chalky print

This technique is a brilliant way to add colour to a large drawing and it creates a really unusual effect. You will need some chalk, pencils and several pieces of paper.

● Draw a simple outline with colouring pencils. For instance, you could draw a rainbow, a butterfly, or just some interesting shapes or doodles.

● Now cover a whole sheet of paper with chalk. Use lots of different colours, but be sure to pick the brightest ones. The chalk needs to be thickly applied, so you might have to draw over the same spot a few times to get the best result.

● Gently place the chalk picture on top of your pencil drawing, with the chalk side facing down, onto your drawing.

● Rub over the back of the chalk picture with your hand to transfer the chalk to your drawing.

● Carefully lift up the chalk paper to reveal your multi-coloured print.

make some scratch art

The fun of making this scratch-art project is almost better than the finished picture! You will need some pencils, a wax crayon, some paper and a few toothpicks.

● Begin by covering an entire sheet of paper with coloured pencil scribbles. Use lots of different colours to make this part as bright and colourful as possible.

● Now cover all of the paper with a thick layer of dark crayon.

● Use a toothpick to scratch away the crayon in different areas to reveal the colourful paper underneath. You can either scratch out patterns or use the toothpick to draw objects, such as stars.

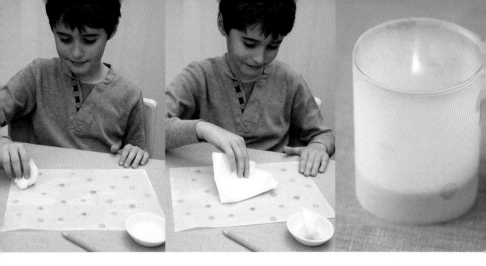

63 create see-through art

This technique will help you create see-through drawings that look amazing when they are displayed on glass. You will need pencils, baby oil, a dry cloth and a cottonball.

- Draw a picture onto a piece of paper. Something simple like flowers, stars or polka dots will work best.

- Carefully pour some of the baby oil into a saucer, dip in the cottonball and then rub it all over the paper. The oil will make the paper transparent.

- Wipe off any excess oil with a dry cloth, by wiping the cloth across the paper. Be careful to do this gently, or you might accidentally rip the paper.

- Display your see-through drawing in a window or wrap it around a glass jar to create a candle holder.

colour your family

Have you ever wondered how your little sister would look with orange hair? This project allows you to colour in your family in any way you like.

● Ask an adult to print you a black and white copy of your favourite family photograph on drawing paper.

● Use bright pencils to colour in the picture. Have fun with it – perhaps give everyone impossible hair colours (like purple) or unusual clothes, or maybe a pirate hat or two. Colour in the background too, if you like.

This is a great way to make birthday or Christmas cards, because you can apply the technique to any photos.

65

draw an optical illusion

Everyone loves optical illusions and this one looks much more complicated than it really is. All you need is some paper, a ruler and some colouring pencils.

● Use a pencil and ruler to draw a square grid onto your paper.

● Now draw shapes (such as hearts, stars and triangles) on top of the grid lines, letting them spread into several squares.

● Colour in the squares outside the shapes. Then colour in the parts of squares inside your shapes using different colours. It will look like the shapes are changing the colour of the squares!

66

draw with erasers

In this project you will be making shapes by drawing with an eraser. The 'rubbed out bits' are the ones you want! You will need paper, colouring pencils and an eraser.

- Colour in a whole piece of paper using your colouring pencils.

- Now use your eraser to rub out the pencil in a few places. You can draw shapes or write messages. Experiment with different sized erasers, if you have some.

- Once you have rubbed out as much as you want, try outlining a few of your erased images with dark pencils to make them stand out more. Which do you like best?

Experiment with different coloured paper, too. For instance, try using yellow paper coloured over with dark blue pencil, then erase star shapes to create the night sky.

Another good shape to experiment with is a flower. Draw the outline then smudge the drawing to add petals.

smudge it on purpose

It can be upsetting to smudge a drawing that you have been working on for a long time, but it's fun to try smudging one on purpose. You will need some paper, a soft pencil and… your fingers!

Draw a picture of someone's head. Now use your fingers to smudge the pencil from the head upwards to add hair. Then smudge inwards from the chin to create a beard. Smudge away until you have created a fantastic face!

make a placemat

It's good to use your art in practical ways, so why not try making some placemats? You could personalise them for each member of the family, or make several with one theme, such as outer space. You will need some white card, colouring pencils and sticky-back, clear plastic.

- Use the bright pencils to draw a picture onto each card. You could draw each family member's favourite food, for instance. Or you could draw a picture of each family member, so they all know where they should be sitting.

- When you have finished your drawing, cover both sides with sticky-back plastic or ask an adult to laminate it, to make your placemat easy to wipe and longer-lasting.

- Cut off any excess plastic and offer to set the table!

You could also turn your placemats into puzzles by drawing hidden objects in busy scenes and challenging people to find them.

spin some pencil art

You can create art in so many different ways, but this is definitely one of the most fun. You will need paper, a CD, a CD spindle, scissors and some coloured pencils.

- Place a CD on a piece of paper and draw around it.

- Use scissors to cut out the circle shape.

- Gently fold the circle in half and cut a small hole into the middle.

- Place the circle onto the CD spindle.

- Put one hand on the spindle and use it to spin the paper around while you hold a crayon onto the paper with your other hand. As you spin, you will create lots of amazing patterns.

use dust for drawing

The part of the pencil that draws the picture – which is sometimes called the 'lead' – can also be used in a different way. Find out how to draw with dust using these easy instructions. All you need is a tissue or handkerchief, some paper and some colouring pencils.

● Use your fingernail to scrape some dust from your pencil tip into a little coloured pile.

● Put the tissue or handkerchief over your finger, dip it into the pencil dust and use your finger to draw a picture with the pencil dust.

● Fill the whole paper with an interesting pattern. The more dust you use, the stronger the colour will be. You can even blend colours together in this way to create new colours. Experiment to find out what else you can do with pencil dust.

pencil stuff

It is always fun to be creative, but there are a few things to keep in mind to make sure you stay safe when doing and making things with pencils.

General safety tips
• Pencils have pointy tips. Be careful not to point them at anyone's face, including your own.
• Never run while holding a pencil.
• Never use pencils as a weapon, not even for a pretend fight.
• Do not draw on anything without asking an adult first.

• Scissors are sharp – only use them with an adult around.
• Always ask an adult for permission before using anything for your crafts. Something you might think is fine to use might still be needed by someone else!
• Never go outside without asking an adult first and make sure to tell them where you are going.
• When exploring outside, remember to take home everything that you brought with you. Always leave nature exactly how you found it.

Different types of pencils
There are many different types of pencils and some are better for one thing, while others may be better for another. It can be hard to remember which types are best, so this handy list might be useful.

Graphite pencils are the grey pencils you use for writing and sketching. They are easy to erase if things go wrong. These pencils are actually a mixture of clay and graphite, and they are divided into two types: 'H' pencils are higher in clay, so they are harder and make lighter marks on paper; while 'B' pencils have more graphite than clay, so they are softer and blacker.

Colouring pencils are not expensive and they come in about 50 different colours (though 12 colours is probably all you need).

Watercolour pencils feel very soft when you draw with them. You can use them just like other coloured pencils, or you can carefully paint water onto the drawn marks to make them look painted.

Crayons are made of wax and colour, and they are great for creating bold lines and colouring in large areas thickly and quickly.

Look after your craft items

It is important to look after all your craft supplies really well to make sure they will last a long time.

• Store your pencils with their tips pointing up so the tips don't break.

• Regularly clean erasers by rubbing them over a blank piece of paper until all the marks on them have gone.

• Remember to put the lid back onto your glue or glue stick after you have finished using it.

• If your glue stick gets dirty or dries out, ask an adult to carefully slice a thin layer of glue off the top to reveal a fresh, clean layer underneath.

• Keep your scissors out of the reach of younger children.

index

animals 36, 60, 96
arty hair clip 73

bark rubbings 13
birds
  feed the birds game 30–1
  nature walks 17
board games 48
boats 20

cards
  cookie-cutter cards 54
  valentines 62
CDs, spinning pencil art 121
chalky prints 109
circles, doodles in 91
clothes, paper people 72
clouds 22
coin pictures 77
collages
  crazy collages 45
  friendship collages 56
colouring pencils 125
colours
  colour your family 113
  optical illusions 114
  roll-a-colour game 32
cookie-cutter cards 54
covering pencils 76
craft supplies 6–7, 125
crayons 110, 125

daydreams, drawing 98

doodles 86
  in circles 91
  doodle game 27
dot games
  dots and boxes 28
  dot-to-dot puzzles 52
  sprouts 38
drawings
  chalky prints 109
  daydreams 98
  doodles 86
  doodles in circles 91
  drawing the other half 96
  drawing with dust 123
  drawing with erasers 116
  favourite things 99
  heads, bodies, feet game
    36–7
  hidden pictures 44
  houses 90
  mandalas 100
  maps 88
  mazes 85
  mini movie 82–3
  nature walks 17
  placemats 118
  plant-pot markers 47
  portraits 92
  quick-on-the-draw 29
  scratch art 110
  secret drawings 63
  see-through art 112
  smudging drawings 117

taking turns 42
3D drawings 95
dressing mini paper people
  72
dust, drawing with 123

equipment 6–7, 124–5
erasers 125
  drawing with 116
  as paint stamps 104

fairy folk 19
family, colouring 113
favourite things 99
feed the birds game 30–1
flowers, pressed 11, 19
fortune-teller 34–5
frames 64

games 24–39
  board games 48
  crazy collages 45
  doodle game 27
  dot-to-dot puzzles 52
  dots and boxes 28
  feed the birds 30–1
  fortune-teller 34–5
  hangman 26
  heads, bodies, feet 36–7
  pick-up sticks 39
  quick-on-the-draw 29
  roll-a-colour game 32
  sprouts 38

glue sticks 7, 125
graphite pencils 125

hair clips 73
hangman 26
happiness journals 99
heads, bodies, feet game 36–7
hidden pictures 44
houses, drawing 90

illusions 95, 114

journals, happiness 99

leaf rubbings 13

magical fairy folk 19
mandalas, drawing 100
maps 51, 88
markers, plant-pot 47
mats 118
mazes 85
menus 53
mini windmills 14–15
mirror pictures 87
modelling clay, pencil sculpture 69
mosaics 78
movie, mini 82–3

natural materials 7
nature walks 17
notebooks 7, 22

optical illusions 114

paint stamps, erasers as 104
paper 7
    covering pencils 76
    notebooks 22
paper people 72
paper 'you' 71

pebbles, pictures on 18
pencils 124–5
    boats 20
    covering 76
    hair clips 73
    mini windmills 14–15
    mosaics 78
    pencil pots 66
    pencil-shaving craft 106–7
    pencil toppers 60
    pick-up sticks 39
    picture frames 64
    sculpture 69
    spinning tops 68
    travel holders 74
    valentines 62
    weaving with 65
pick-up sticks 39
picture frames 64
pictures
    chalky prints 109
    coin pictures 77
    colour your family 113
    daydreams 98
    drawing the other half 96
    flower pictures 11
    hidden pictures 44
    magical fairy folk 19
    mirror pictures 87
    pencil-shaving craft 106–7
    stone pictures 18
placemats 118
plant-pot markers 47
portraits 92
pots, pencil 66
pressed flowers 11, 19
prints, chalky 109
promises 50

quick-on-the-draw 29

recycled materials 7
restaurant menus 53

roll-a-colour game 32
rubbings, leaf and bark 13

safety 6, 124
scissors 7, 124, 125
scratch art 110
sculpture 69
secret drawings 63
secret messages 76
see-through art 112
shavings, pencil 106–7
smudging drawings 117
spinning pencil art 121
spinning tops 68
sprouts game 38
stamping, with erasers 104
stone pictures 18
string, weaving 65

taking turns 42
3D drawings 95
toppers, pencil 60
tops, spinning 68
travel holders 74
treasure maps 51
triangles, doodles in circles 91

valentines 62
viewfinders 10

walks, nature 17
watercolour pencils 125
wax crayons 110, 125
weaving with pencils 65
windmills, mini 14–15
wool, weaving 65
word games 26

'you', paper 71

acknowledgments

Thank you to all the children who took part in the photography for this book and made the photoshoot such a success: Oliver Crook, Jessica Everett, Sam Everett, Rafferty Figueira, Billy Goodridge, Oliver Goodridge, Charlie Killick, Madison McDonnell, Tatianna McDonnell, Lois Patel and Emily Scantlebury.

Thanks to Natalie McHugh for the use of her house as a location for the photography.

Thanks to Sara Everett for the wonderful photography and great location.

Produced for Frances Lincoln by Tracy Killick Art Direction and Design and www.editorsonline.org

Commissioning Editor: Sarah Tomley
Art Director: Tracy Killick
Proofreader: Louise Abbott